DEALING WITH E-MAIL

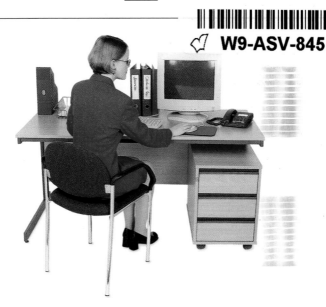

DAVID BRAKE

LONDON, NEW YORK, MUNICH,
MELBOURNE, AND DELHI

Project Editor Nicky Munro
US Editor Margaret Parrish
DTP Designer Rajen Shah
Production Controller Kevin Ward
Managing Editor Adèle Hayward
Managing Art Editor Karen Self
Category Publisher Stephanie Jackson

DK DELHI

Project Editor Ranjana Sengupta
Editor Rimli Borooah
Project Art Editor Kavita Dutta
DTP Designer Balwant Singh
Managing Editor Ira Pande
Managing Art Editor Aparna Sharma
Editorial Consultant Anita Roy

First American Edition 2003
Published in the United States by
DK Publishing, Inc.
375 Hudson Street
New York, New York 10014

03 04 05 06 07 08 10 9 8 7 6 5 4 3 2 1

Copyright © 2003 Dorling Kindersley Limited

A Cataloging-in-Publication record for this book
is available from the Library of Congress

ISBN 0-7894-9539-2

Color reproduction by Colourscan, Singapore

Printed and bound in Hong Kong
by Wing King Tong

See our complete product line at
www.dk.com

CONTENTS

INTRODUCTION

The explosive growth in e-mail use has revolutionized business communication. E-mail provides a cheap, easy-to-use, almost instantaneous way to communicate with people all around the world. However, it also presents new organizational, technical, and legal challenges. Dealing with E-mail uses everyday language to clearly explain the various features of your e-mail software, shows you how to organize your e-mail efficiently and write precise e-mails, and clarifies the legal issues that arise from using e-mail. With 101 practical tips and a self-assessment questionnaire that allows you to evaluate your e-mailing skills, this book will help you discover the benefits that e-mail can bring to your organization, and enable you to employ this communication medium to the full.

TAKING CONTROL IN THE E-MAIL AGE

Today, electronic mail is one of the most important tools of business communication. To take full advantage of its potential, it is essential to learn the most effective ways of using it.

SWITCHING OVER TO E-MAIL

E-mail has become the dominant form of business communication, and the flow of e-mail traffic is increasing constantly. Understand how this technology has changed the face of written communication, and adjust your work practices in response to this.

1 Remember that, like other business activities, e-mail needs management.

REALIZING THE POTENTIAL

E-mail arrived in the world of business in the mid-1990s. However, the first internet e-mail program was created over 20 years earlier, for use by scientists and the military. Businesses and consumers soon grasped the internet's importance, especially for e-mailing, which has been its most popular function from the start.

◀ **CHOOSING E-MAIL**
There are now over half a billion e-mail mailboxes functioning globally. Across most of the industrialized world, the number of e-mails exceeds the number of items sent by mail.

CREATING A NEW CULTURE

The differences between e-mail and regular post are vast. E-mail is an increasingly popular medium of communication, which is changing business vocabulary, ways of working, and expectations. It is fast, cheap, and easy to send, so you can write a quick line to someone around the world without having to print out a letter, find an envelope and the correct postage, sign, seal, and mail it. The speed and simplicity has encouraged a new informality in communications, even in a business context.

▲ DISSOLVING DISTANCES
With the advent of the internet and e-mail, computer users have information from all over the world at their fingertips.

2 Encourage all your business contacts to work with e-mail.

METCALFE'S LAW

Robert Metcalfe, the inventor of Ethernet, a type of local area network, formulated a simple law to explain the explosion in the use of e-mail. The law states that the utility, or usefulness, of e-mail rises sharply as the number of users increases. This accounts for the phenomenal growth of e-mail in the world in the last few years. Today in the professional world there is hardly any business that does not have an e-mail address. This stage of "critical mass" has led to a chain reaction all over the world as increasing numbers of e-mail users sign up each day.

Utility

Utility = Users^2

Users

▲ UNDERSTANDING THE GROWTH OF E-MAIL
As more people use e-mail, non-users have more reason to sign up and there is a rise in demand. This further increases the utility of e-mail.

UNDERSTANDING E-MAIL

E-mail programs are packed with several linked features to fulfill the needs of interactive communication. Acquaint yourself with these features and understand how e-mails are transmitted to make optimum use of this medium.

3 Be aware that there are some risks involved in sending e-mail.

4 Use a modern e-mail program for compatibility.

TRANSMITTING E-MAILS

If you send an e-mail to a colleague in the same office on the same e-mail system, the path is simple. The e-mail is sent to a central computer—the mail server. Your colleague, who is connected to the same server, is notified and opens the message. E-mail sent via the internet is passed from your server, via a chain of servers across the internet, to another server closer to your intended recipient. In theory, an e-mail could be intercepted and read, or even lost, at any point in this chain.

▼ **SENDING AN E-MAIL VIA THE INTERNET**
E-mail travels from the sender's computer to the Internet Service Provider (ISP) and via internet mail servers to the recipient's ISP.

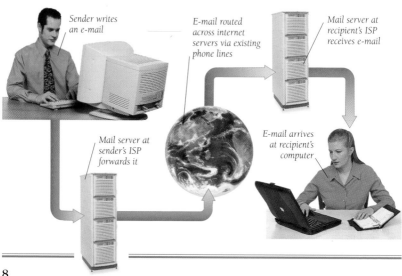

Sender writes an e-mail

E-mail routed across internet servers via existing phone lines

Mail server at recipient's ISP receives e-mail

Mail server at sender's ISP forwards it

E-mail arrives at recipient's computer

ANALYZING COMMON E-MAIL FEATURES

An e-mail message contains the same basic features, no matter which program you are using. These features allow you to carry out all the functions of traditional business correspondence in a much more efficient way, since it has the speed of electronic communication. Other advanced features allow you to, among other things, file addresses automatically, forward messages to others, and search for sent or received mail.

5 File the address of an e-mail by clicking on it.

6 Use "Bcc" to avoid revealing other peoples' e-mail addresses.

▼ **USING FUNCTIONS EFFECTIVELY**

Your e-mail program is packed with useful functions to make communication easy. Familiarize yourself with all the key features to use e-mail at its full potential.

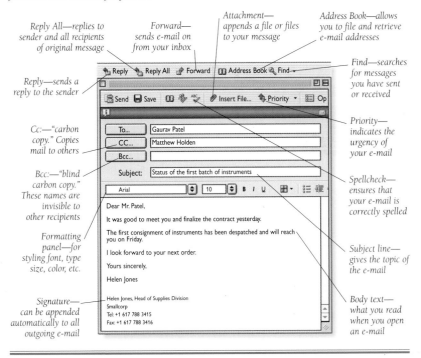

Reply All—replies to sender and all recipients of original message

Forward— sends e-mail on from your inbox

Attachment— appends a file or files to your message

Address Book—allows you to file and retrieve e-mail addresses

Find—searches for messages you have sent or received

Reply—sends a reply to the sender

Cc:—"carbon copy." Copies mail to others

Bcc:—"blind carbon copy." These names are invisible to other recipients

Formatting panel—for styling font, type size, color, etc.

Signature— can be appended automatically to all outgoing e-mail

Priority— indicates the urgency of your e-mail

Spellcheck— ensures that your e-mail is correctly spelled

Subject line— gives the topic of the e-mail

Body text— what you read when you open an e-mail

EXPLAINING E-MAIL TERMS

TERM	DEFINITION
E-MAIL SERVER	A computer that is responsible for storing and managing all the e-mail for a work group or organization.
ENCRYPTION	The process of "scrambling" a message so that only the recipients who know the correct password can read it.
FILTER	A tool in most e-mail software that lets you file e-mail into folders or perform other functions automatically. Sometimes called a "rule."
HTML E-MAIL	Messages that include formatting or images. They often look like web pages. Some e-mail packages cannot receive HTML messages.
INTERNET	The global network of interconnected computers that communicate with each other via the existing telecommunications networks.
INTRANET	Web pages and other internet-style services that are only accessible from inside your organization.
ISP	Internet Service Provider. A company that provides businesses or individuals with access to the internet through phone lines or direct connection.
KEYWORD	A word that you use to search for an e-mail, piece of text, or web page—normally one as distinctive as possible to exclude unrelated material.
RETURN RECEIPT	A feature that can be activated to send you a message when the recipient receives and opens your e-mail.
SPAM	Unsolicited commercial e-mail, often offering illegal or objectionable products. Senders of spam are known as "spammers."
THREAD	A succession of e-mails (or messageboard postings) that relate to a single subject.

CALCULATING THE COST OF E-MAIL

Although sending e-mail—particularly within an office network—seems to be cost-free, it is important to recognize that the true cost of even traditional mail was never just the cost of the stamp, ink, and paper. As the formula below explains, e-mail's main cost is in time—the time spent to compose it, read it, and file it. In many organizations, it is as easy to send an e-mail to 100 people as to one, but the cost may be very high. An irrelevant e-mail sent to 100 people in an office may take just a minute for each of the recipients to scan it and discard it, but it still wastes over an hour-and-a-half of working time.

7 Request an automatic receipt to the e-mails that you send.

8 Double-check e-mail addresses when you enter them by hand.

| Time spent as fraction of average wage per day | X | Number of employees in the organization | X | Number of working days per year | = | Annual loss of productivity to the organization |

▲ COSTING LOW-PRIORITY E-MAIL
The cost to an organization of time spent on nonessential e-mail can be worked out by estimating the time an average employee spends reading it every day.

THINGS TO DO

1. Acknowledge receipt of an important e-mail.
2. Use your address book to access the correct address.
3. Match the subject line to the text of your e-mail.

UNDERSTANDING WHY E-MAIL MAY NOT ARRIVE

The most common reason for an e-mail not being delivered is that it was addressed incorrectly. E-mail sent via the internet is transferred between several e-mail servers along the way. It is possible, but rare, for one of the machines in the chain between you and the recipient to crash and fail to pass on your e-mail. Also, the recipient's e-mail software may reject your message because it is too large or because it believes it to be "spam." Normally, you will be sent an e-mail telling you when one of these events has occurred, but this may take hours to arrive or even fail to arrive at all. Always ask the recipient to send an acknowledgment of e-mails that are important.

USING E-MAIL EFFECTIVELY

All e-mail programs have built-in features designed to make your use of the medium fast, easy, and efficient. These are helpful, but for optimum e-mail performance they must be utilized in conjunction with sensible work practices.

9 Keep in mind that not every e-mail you receive needs an immediate reply.

10 Avoid checking your inbox every five minutes.

11 Set aside a fixed time each day to reply to e-mail.

PRIORITIZING RESPONSES

Making the best use of the tools your e-mail software provides makes the job of dealing with e-mails much quicker. Organize your messages by prioritizing them appropriately. Not all e-mails need an instant response—and some can be replied to with pre-written text. Many e-mails do not require a response, and others can safely be deleted from your mailbox without being read at all. Ask colleagues, customers, and suppliers to indicate the urgency of their e-mails and any deadline for your response.

▼ RATING E-MAILS
Learn to organize the e-mails that are in your inbox in order of their importance and urgency and deal with them accordingly.

	High Urgency	Low Urgency
High Importance	**Respond immediately**	**Make time in your day to respond**
Low Importance	**Respond only if high-importance e-mail has been dealt with first**	**Question necessity, delegate, or, if necessary, ignore**

Avoiding E-mail

E-mail is rapidly replacing oral communication, even among people in the same office. However, a phone call or even a chat is often more effective than an e-mail. When an e-mail is necessary, remember that copying in too many people can often lead to pointless discussions. If you find that you are constantly receiving e-mails that have no relevance to your area of work (for example, if you are on a standard company mailing list), use the "ignore mail from" feature on your e-mail program to stop such mail coming into your mailbox.

▲ TALKING IT OVER
A quick word with key colleagues often resolves an issue more easily—and quickly—than several rounds of e-mail, with whole departments copied in.

12 Make all routine announcements via an intranet where available.

Using Special Software

Certain advanced e-mail programs are available to perform specific tasks. "Contact management" or "Customer relationship management" software, aimed at sales and support teams, stores information about clients alongside their e-mail addresses and reminds users to send messages on clients' birthdays and anniversaries, or to chase progress on projects at regular intervals. "Workflow" software can automate the flow of e-mail within an organization, so that invoices, for example, can be authorized and forwarded with a single click of the mouse.

▲ AUTOMATING TASKS
You need not depend on your planner to remember things to do. Advanced software can now do the work for you.

CHANGING THE WAY YOU WORK

O ne of the most profound effects of e-mail has been to change the way people work. The ability to send and receive messages, along with attached documents from anywhere, without using a phone line, has led to an increase in out-of-office work.

13 Check if your cell phone can receive e-mail abroad before you travel.

14 Use a cell phone or PDA for e-mailing while you are traveling.

▼ **OPTIMIZING DOWNTIME**
Commuting time can be usefully spent checking your inbox and dealing with your e-mail messages.

USING E-MAIL ON THE MOVE

Until recently, you had to plug a laptop in to a phone line to pick up your e-mail. Now, with high transmission cellular phone links and growing wireless networks, you can receive e-mail wherever you are. Personal Digital Assistants (PDAs) can also be used to connect to e-mail. However, it usually costs more to pick up e-mail this way, and some of these devices cannot always read the attachments that accompany an e-mail.

WORKING FROM HOME

E-mail enables people to work from home more effectively while staying in touch with the office. This reduces office costs, since several employees can share a single desk (known as "hot-desking"). Workers—particularly those with young children—value the flexibility that working from home offers. Using e-mail to facilitate this can help organizations to keep key staff motivated. Team members can work together on a project even when they are at home.

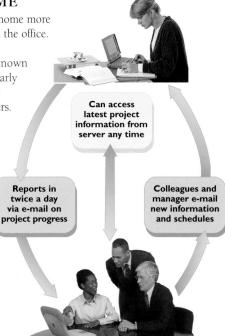

Can access latest project information from server any time

Reports in twice a day via e-mail on project progress

Colleagues and manager e-mail new information and schedules

MAINTAINING ▶ INFORMATION FLOW
Updates and other information can be exchanged between the office and your home almost instantaneously.

15 Examine how e-mail can help you work flexible hours.

REDEFINING ▶ WORK PRACTICES
In this example, e-mail offered the manager a convenient way to stay in touch with colleagues and deal promptly with routine jobs when she was out of office on work-related tasks.

CASE STUDY

A marketing manager had to spend long periods out of the office attending trade fairs and meeting advertising agencies and potential clients. Because of the time she spent on the move and away from her desk, she was finding it difficult to liaise with other departments in the company. She bought a cellular phone with a built-in modem, and the necessary equipment to connect it to a laptop. Now, when she is with clients, she is not interrupted by calls to her cell phone. Instead, she keeps up with her colleagues by e-mail when she has free time throughout the day, wherever she is across the country—whether in the evening after meetings, or on a train. Consequently, when she returns to the office, she has already dealt with routine administration and is aware of all the issues she has to tackle.

CHOOSING BETWEEN E-MAIL AND OTHER MEDIA

Compared with other methods of communication, e-mail has many advantages. Once you understand fully how e-mail can be used to serve your needs and those of your organization, it will become a resource that you cannot work without.

16 Use e-mail to set up meetings and circulate the agenda in advance.

17 Attach graphics to help clarify a complex message.

ADDING UP THE BENEFITS

For the cost of an internet connection you can send an e-mail to anyone with an e-mail address anywhere in the world. Pictures and text files can also be attached to the message. E-mail can be sent at any time, easing difficulties caused by global time differences, and can be opened at the convenience of the recipient. Unlike phone calls, both the sender and recipient can easily file and retrieve what has been sent and received.

COMPARING DIFFERENT METHODS OF COMMUNICATION

TYPE	COST	DATA RECALL
E-MAIL	Low—once you are connected, e-mail costs very little.	Excellent—e-mail is automatically stored and is easy to relocate.
TELEPHONE CALL	Variable—depends on charges and whether it is a conference call involving several people.	Variable—recording and transcribing calls is expensive. Minutes are rarely complete.
FACE-TO-FACE MEETING	High—disruption of work schedules and possible travel and accommodation costs.	Variable—as with a telephone call, keeping an accurate record is time-consuming.

KNOWING THE PITFALLS

The cost to the recipient of an e-mail can be much higher than the cost to the sender—a single person can waste the time of several people with a long message. Because e-mail seems more private than a phone call, employees are often tempted to use it for personal messages. Another danger is the temptation to reply to e-mails as soon as they are received, because the recipient feels it will only take a second or two to deal with—this can disrupt work flow.

SIMPLIFYING TASKS

One of the revolutionary effects of e-mail is the ease with which you can communicate with many external contacts and customers. However, e-mail does not fundamentally change the internal processes of most businesses. It sometimes replaces office memos and can act as a substitute for phone calls and meetings. E-mail is very useful for conveying factual information, but is less effective at persuading people.

Eye contact and body language conveys a point persuasively

TALKING FACE TO FACE ▶
Within an office or in the same city, meetings can work more effectively than an exchange of e-mail.

TIMING	INFLUENCE
Manageable—even an e-mail sent when the recipient is out of the office can be read on the recipient's return.	Low—important audible and visual cues are missing. If sent to multiple recipients, it is hard to make each feel exclusively addressed.
Problematic—the timing should suit both the callers, especially if time zones are far apart. Conference calls need very careful scheduling.	Medium—your tone can convey enthusiasm and you can plan what you say carefully. However, your physical presence is missing.
Problematic—participants who have traveled a long way can feel at a disadvantage if they have not had time to adjust before the meeting.	High—the trouble taken to set it up encourages people to resolve issues. Body language and tone of voice help to reinforce what you say.

MANAGING E-MAIL EFFICIENTLY

The way you manage your e-mail affects your efficiency at work. Learn to make optimum use of your e-mail software so that it saves you time and helps you to be more organized.

ORGANIZING YOUR MAILBOX

As e-mail takes over from the office memo, your mailbox can be just as important as your filing cabinet. To keep all important messages at your fingertips, use multiple folders and employ filters so that your e-mail is automatically filed into the correct folder.

| 18 | Use public folders to allow e-mails to be viewed by all team members. |

GETTING ORGANIZED

> Create folders for each project

> Create subfolders, if necessary, for each folder

> File all incoming or sent e-mail in relevant folder or sub-folder

CREATING MULTIPLE E-MAIL FOLDERS

All your incoming mail is stored in the inbox, and outgoing mail in the "Sent Items" folder. This is equivalent to having just two electronic filing trays marked "In" and "Out." If you receive a lot of e-mails and leave them all in your inbox, it can be difficult and time-consuming to locate specific e-mails when you need them. Create appropriate folders into which you can move messages to be stored. Of course, it is possible to search for e-mail by keyword, but the search is much faster if you have narrowed it down to a single area.

PLANNING AHEAD

Instead of creating new folders as you go, think carefully beforehand about the best way to organize the e-mail you are likely to get. If you have some folders for people, others for projects, and some sorted by subject, it becomes increasingly difficult to decide where a message belongs. Most e-mail packages will allow you to have folders within folders so that you can divide e-mail into—for example—work and personal, and within those, into different projects.

19 Encourage everyone who is in your team to adopt the same e-mail filing system.

POINTS TO REMEMBER

● Organize your e-mail folders according to your projects.

● An e-mail should be deleted as soon as you have dealt with it.

● Only necessary e-mails should be stored in your system to avoid clogging up your mailbox.

● Your filing system should be clear—others may need to find an e-mail in your mailbox.

▼ KEEPING YOUR FILES IN ORDER
Categorize your e-mails into clearly labeled folders according to subject and priority. Check the folders regularly to file new mail and delete outdated messages.

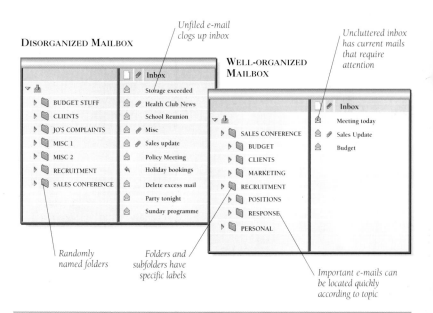

Unfiled e-mail clogs up inbox

DISORGANIZED MAILBOX

Uncluttered inbox has current mails that require attention

WELL-ORGANIZED MAILBOX

Randomly named folders

Folders and subfolders have specific labels

Important e-mails can be located quickly according to topic

FILING E-MAILS AUTOMATICALLY

Most programs can organize your e-mail by an automatic process, so you do not need to file it by hand. They do this by examining each e-mail as it comes in, and consulting a set of filters that you set up. For example, all e-mails with a given subject line or from a particular project team can automatically be sent to the folder of your choice. Or any e-mail that contains a certain phrase such as "invoice payable" can be replied to with a standard reply or forwarded to the right person without your lifting a finger.

▼ ORGANIZING FOLDERS
Treat your mailbox like a filing cabinet and organize your folders based on your work requirements.

As with any efficient filing system, your e-mail should be in main folders and subfolders to find messages easily

QUESTIONS TO ASK YOURSELF

Q Do all e-mails from a person or company belong in the same folder?

Q Do I ensure that I regularly read through the messages that are automatically filed?

Q Are my e-mails being filed in the right folders?

Q Can I discard old filters that I set up earlier?

Q Are there any recently unused folders that I could remove?

SETTING UP FILTERS

If you find that you are dealing with many e-mails at once, make note of how you do it. Do you file all e-mail from a certain group of people to one place? Do you find you are sending similar replies to anyone who e-mails with a sales inquiry? If so, and you are able to identify the pattern, you can set up a filter that will automatically do that task for you from now on. In most cases, you can also apply this filter retroactively to the e-mail you have already received. Some web-based e-mail services and e-mail packages use similar techniques to ensure you do not receive "spam."

20 Take the time to organize e-mails now—it saves time later.

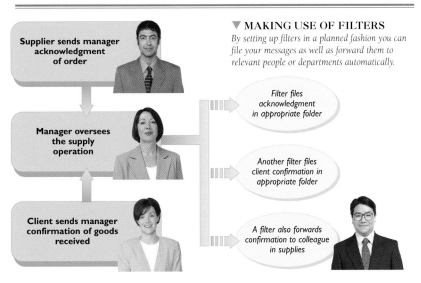

▼ MAKING USE OF FILTERS
By setting up filters in a planned fashion you can file your messages as well as forward them to relevant people or departments automatically.

Supplier sends manager acknowledgment of order

Manager oversees the supply operation

Client sends manager confirmation of goods received

Filter files acknowledgment in appropriate folder

Another filter files client confirmation in appropriate folder

A filter also forwards confirmation to colleague in supplies

MONITORING FILTERS

When you are setting up filters, remember that they will not always work as you intended. Someone from accounts may e-mail you with a question about personnel issues, or your partner may e-mail you a file you need from home, only for it to be filed under "personal." Do not assume that your e-mail is being filed correctly. Look through the filters you have created every few months to ensure, for example, that you are not automatically filing mail from people no longer working in the organization. Too many filters operating at once may slow down the display of incoming messages while your computer works out where to file them.

21 Check for wrongly filed messages in your less-used folders.

▼ KEEPING TABS
You need to keep track of the filters you have set up. Retain only those filters that are filing, forwarding, or deleting e-mail as you intended.

Set up filters

Check filters regularly

Remove unnecessary filters

FINDING E-MAILS

As you rely more on e-mail, and as more and more of it piles up in your mailbox, it can be difficult to find the messages that you need quickly, even if they are organized into folders. Use the tools in your e-mail package to make this task easier.

22 Remember, you can search for sent, as well as received, e-mail.

23 Delete or archive old e-mail to find current e-mail more easily.

▼ **ORGANIZING THE INBOX**
A well-ordered inbox allows you to find an important e-mail at a moment's notice and helps to save time.

SCANNING YOUR MAILBOX

Locating files becomes easier when you have divided your e-mails into topics and filed them in different mailboxes. If you know the approximate date of the e-mail, its subject, or the sender's name, you can instantly sort your mailbox by that criterion—normally by clicking on an appropriate button above each field. Unread e-mail is often highlighted with a bold font and a symbol (such as a closed envelope). This helps you to spot forgotten e-mails as you scan down the list of mails in your inbox.

Colleague asks for details of an agreement

Looks at "Received" list and finds the relevant e-mail quickly

LOCATING AN E-MAIL

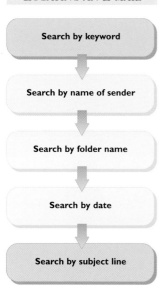

Search by keyword

Search by name of sender

Search by folder name

Search by date

Search by subject line

24 Switch to another task while you wait for the keyword search to finish.

SEARCHING BY KEYWORD

All e-mail software includes a "Find" facility. If you select it, a box will appear on your screen, into which you can type a word or words that you know are contained in the message that you want to locate. Just typing in a single keyword and hoping for the best may be quite frustrating, especially if you have a lot of e-mail messages in one place and the only words you have to go by are common ones such as "budget" or "sales." Spend a moment to be specific—it will speed up your search considerably.

USING ADVANCED SEARCHES

If you are presented with a simple space to enter a keyword, look for an "advanced search" option. If you know that the message you are looking for was sent by a certain person or within a given month, or would be in a particular folder, you can usually add these parameters to your search using the appropriate boxes and buttons. You can also look for messages with a certain priority label, such as "urgent." Alternately, if you know that the keyword you are looking for is in the subject line, you can indicate that in your search instead of searching the entire text of the message.

DOS AND DON'TS

✔ Do use at least two criteria, such as the date and a keyword, to make your search more effective.

✔ Do choose a word specific to the e-mail you are looking for.

✘ Don't leave a large number of unsorted mails in your inbox.

✘ Don't use a "simple" search across all e-mail if you have specific information to narrow your search.

25 Think of the most unusual relevant keyword when you are using "Find."

Avoiding E-mail Overload

You can use technology to help you deal with e-mails you send, but the way you manage the e-mails you receive is just as important. Learn how to recognize e-mails that you can safely ignore or delegate in order to free up your time.

26 Make sure that you only send a reply to those who need it.

27 Delete all unnecessary e-mails you receive as soon as possible.

DELEGATING RESPONSIBILITY

If an e-mail you receive can be handled by someone else, forward it to them and copy in the sender to inform them that someone else is now dealing with their request. If you regularly receive enquiries about matters that are not within your sphere of responsibility, use filters to forward the e-mails with a note to the colleague to whom you think you can delegate the work.

▼ **PROCESSING INQUIRIES**

E-mail allows the client's inquiry to be forwarded to the relevant person in the organization, while the client is kept informed of the process at every stage.

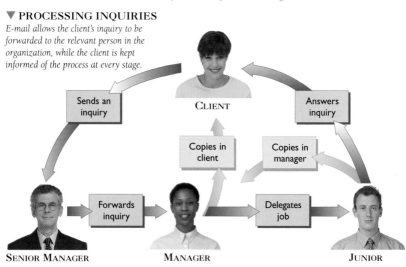

Sends an inquiry

CLIENT

Answers inquiry

Copies in client

Copies in manager

Forwards inquiry

Delegates job

SENIOR MANAGER

MANAGER

JUNIOR

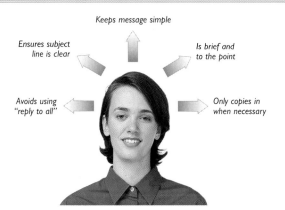

Keeps message simple

Ensures subject line is clear

Is brief and to the point

Avoids using "reply to all"

Only copies in when necessary

◀ **BEING CONSIDERATE**
Treat your colleagues the way you would like to be treated yourself. Avoid long and frequent e-mails—that way they will get back to you only when necessary, and not out of habit.

KNOWING WHEN NOT TO RESPOND

Sometimes you will be included in an e-mail exchange as a courtesy—perhaps to make sure you are aware of some activity. If your name appears on the "Cc" recipient list, this is usually a sign that your input is not required—resist the temptation to get drawn into the conversation. You may also sometimes suspect you have been copied into a discussion in error. If you are in doubt, check with the person who sent you the message in the first place, before getting involved, to see what, if anything, is expected of you.

28 Label e-mails that you will need to refer to later.

29 Inform people if you think they are sending you e-mails in error.

AVOIDING REPEATED READING

One of the most common mistakes is to leave old e-mail lying around in your mailbox. Usually, urgent e-mail tends to get replied to quickly, while unimportant e-mails get deleted. However, e-mail that falls between these two categories can linger for months, being read occasionally but never acted upon. Once you have looked at an e-mail, try to act on it right away. If you must return to it later, use your e-mail software's labeling feature to indicate a deadline for action, or at least how urgent it is, so you do not need to keep going back and rereading it.

KNOWING WHEN TO DEAL WITH E-MAIL

Although e-mail can be dealt with instantly, it does not have to be. Unless you are expecting urgent e-mail, leave your e-mail program switched off until you have dealt with the day's most important issues. When you do scan through the inbox, do not bother reading past the subject line of low-priority messages unless you have the time to deal with them. Tackle important e-mails first and leave the rest for later. Many e-mails will be rendered irrelevant by time or subsequent messages.

QUESTIONS TO ASK YOURSELF

Q Do I need to read this e-mail now, or can it wait?

Q Is this e-mail someone else's responsibility?

Q Does the sender of this message expect an answer from me and by when?

Q Could this issue be tackled faster and more effectively with a phone call?

30 Keep both sent and received e-mails to manageable levels.

TACKLING E-MAIL AFTER AN ABSENCE

Scan your e-mail quickly for urgent inquiries

Read backward from your return to your departure

Find a convenient time to process your remaining e-mail

When you have dealt with an e-mail, remove all the earlier ones on the same topic

BEING OUT OF THE OFFICE

There will inevitably be times when you are unable to collect or deal with e-mails. To avoid overflowing mailboxes, arrange for someone to pick up your e-mail in your absence. Try to set up a filter to provide an automatic response to e-mails, with text explaining your absence and informing recipients if their message has been forwarded to another person. If the response will be delayed, give warning. If you cannot provide an automatic response, consider advising those with whom you are in frequent e-mail contact that you will be away—otherwise, they may send you an e-mail expecting a quick response.

31 Use filters that forward e-mail automatically to your colleagues when you are away from office.

DISCOURAGING UNNECESSARY E-MAIL

A great deal of time is spent on nonessential e-mail. Explain to staff and colleagues that messages should only be forwarded when a decision is needed. E-mails routinely addressed to whole departments may often be missed by the people who most need to see them. Discourage joke e-mails, petitions, and chain letters—these clog up inboxes and waste office time. Consider using alternative computer systems—for instance, a messageboard for the announcement of a new employee.

32 Ensure that e-mail is the most efficient way for you to communicate.

Meets colleague at a coffee shop, to talk over project

CATCHING UP ▶
An occasional chat is good for workplace relationships, so make it a point to meet up with colleagues once in a while, rather than always e-mailing them.

USING ELECTRONIC ALTERNATIVES TO E-MAIL

SYSTEM	ADVANTAGES
INTRANET	Allows the company to present key messages to employees in a more structured way. Can be used to make routine announcements.
MESSAGEBOARD	Helps group collaboration since all contributions are accessible and can be easily indexed. Usually found as part of a wider intranet.
INSTANT MESSAGING	Allows instant interchange of short messages with someone who is online. Typically used socially, but businesses may also find it useful.
VIDEOCONFERENCING	Can be organized through the internet or the electronic corporate network using webcams and other special equipment.
GROUPWARE	Software that enables several people to edit and discuss the same document or image simultaneously across a network.

MANAGING YOUR ADDRESS BOOK

Make optimum use of your e-mail program to store and find frequently used addresses. E-mail software can save you from having to find and retype e-mail addresses, and it can speed up the addressing of e-mail you send to groups.

33 Use your e-mail address book to avoid misspelling the address.

34 When e-mailing to many people at once, split the list into smaller parts, or hide addresses with Bcc.

USING THE ADDRESS BOOK EFFECTIVELY

You should consider adding an address to your address book once you have sent several messages to that person. File your contacts' addresses into appropriate folders or categories and assign nicknames to people or groups. Instead of typing "name.surname@thiscompany.com" you can just type "Thiscompany Sales" and your e-mail program will find the right address—better still, you can substitute a short code such as "thisco."

Gives colleague list of key contacts

◀ **SHARING ADDRESSES**
If you are going to be away for a while, write down important addresses from your address book so that no one needs to access your mailbox in your absence.

35 File phone numbers and other details in your address book.

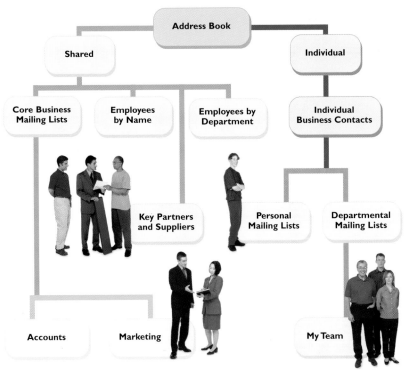

SHARING ADDRESS BOOKS

A central address book ensures that information about new clients or projects is disseminated and that interoffice e-mail is sent to the correct people. Most software aimed at an office environment will have this option—although not all e-mail packages offer it. Some contact information can and should be stored by employees in their private address book, but other address information may be shared through a common mailing list. Ensure that someone is responsible for updating the list, keeping track of people joining or leaving the company, transfers, and promotions.

▲ CREATING PERSONAL ADDRESS BOOK GROUPS

Use software to set up e-mail groups in your address book for people to whom you send the same e-mails repeatedly. You can write to each department or "My Team" without typing in individual addresses.

36 Remember to update names in address book groups regularly.

Finding E-mail Addresses

The internet makes it easy to find most pieces of information, but finding people's e-mail addresses is an exception. There is no single guaranteed method, but it is possible to track someone down even if you do not have their details.

37 Search the shared company address book to trace a lost e-mail address.

Using E-mail Search

If you do not remember an e-mail address, use the "Find" function to locate the mail you exchanged with that person and get the address. Use the company name or person's surname as keywords. If you find an e-mail from someone else in the same company, use that as a guide. For example, if you want to e-mail Henry Smith and find an e-mail from "j.jones@hiscompany.com," it is likely Henry's address is "h.smith@hiscompany.com."

User name or user ID

David.Brake@largecorp.com

Domain name / *Domain name code*

▲ **LOCATING AN ADDRESS**
Once you know what the domain name is, you can usually find a person's e-mail address without much difficulty.

Understanding Domain Name Codes

Domain	Meaning
.com	Usually indicates the sender is a commercial business.
.org	Usually indicates the sender is from a nonprofit organization.
.uk, .cn, etc.	Country code subdomain indicating the country the sender is sending from—the UK and China in these examples.
.gov	Subdomain sometimes, combined with country code to indicate a government agency in that country.
.edu	Subdomain sometimes, combined with country code to indicate an educational institution in that country.

▼ SEARCHING FOR AN E-MAIL ADDRESS

E-mail addresses consist of a user name that is separated by an @
from the domain name code. Trying different combinations of the
user's names and/or initials will help you find the e-mail address.

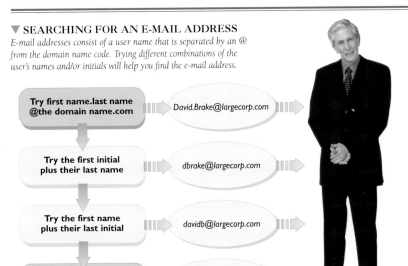

Try first name.last name
@the domain name.com → David.Brake@largecorp.com →

Try the first initial
plus their last name → dbrake@largecorp.com →

Try the first name
plus their last initial → davidb@largecorp.com →

The first name may be
sufficient in a small company → david@smallcorp.com →

CHECKING PUBLIC DATABASES

Public e-mail databases that are available on the internet can be checked when you are looking for an e-mail address, although they may not be of much help. These databases rely on users to enter their addresses, but many people avoid registering, as their addresses can be "looted" by spammers. A regular search engine may also help you to find a person's e-mail address if it is published on the web.

LOCATING AN ORGANIZATION'S WEBSITE

Many organizations have websites with links to specific departments. Some even have details, such as the position of employees in the company. If you know the company name, an internet search engine should take you to the organization website, which you can search. There will be a general e-mail address for the company, which you can use to send a message requesting the address of the person you wish to contact.

38 Confirm that an e-mail address you have located is correct before sending a message.

CUTTING DOWN ON WORK

By planning ahead, you can save yourself a lot of typing when you write e-mails. You can use templates, as you would for letters, and signature files as you would printed stationery. This gives your e-mail correspondence a professional appearance.

39 Make sure you read through a template e-mail before you send it.

CREATING TEMPLATES

Create standard template letters

↓

Copy the text and paste it into an e-mail

↓

Modify each slightly to make them more personal

↓

Send to the recipients

40 Base your template on messages you send frequently.

SETTING UP TEMPLATES

E-mail software normally allows you to generate standard letters just like word processing packages. In its simplest form, it allows you to store the text of an e-mail – a standard opening sales pitch, for example – and send it to others with a click of the mouse. More advanced software can automatically adjust the text of each message according to changes you specify, so that the message can include the name of the recipient's organization, for example. If your software does not have this function, you can save standard texts as word processor files, paste the text into your e-mail, and edit it to make it more personalized.

DOS AND DON'TS

✔ Do read through e-mail you have sent to find repeated messages you can turn into templates.

✔ Do edit a template e-mail before sending to make sure it does not seem generic.

✔ Do re-read your templates periodically to ensure they are not out of date.

✘ Don't use filters to automatically send e-mail using a template, unless necessary, as it can appear impersonal.

✘ Don't use templates for responses where the human touch is important.

✘ Don't include detailed information in a template, if this is likely to change frequently.

41 Check whether your computer's mailmerge function can be used with e-mail.

FORWARDING E-MAIL

You will often receive an e-mail that you cannot deal with without information from someone else. To avoid writing a long explanatory e-mail to your colleague, simply forward the e-mail you have received and insert a short message at the beginning. The subject line will automatically show that it is a forwarded message and will be the same as the original e-mail you have received. If you feel that the subject needs to be clarified, you can easily change the subject line.

USING SIGNATURES

Most e-mail software allows you to append a "signature" automatically to the bottom of every outgoing e-mail. This usually consists of the writer's phone number and company details, a disclaimer that attempts to protect the writer or their company from legal action in the event of a dispute, or occasionally a short humorous phrase or a promotional slogan. Avoid large signature files—it is irritating to receive a one-line message followed by a 20-line signature! Test your signature by sending a message to yourself at another e-mail account or to a colleague to make sure it has come out correctly in the display.

42 Use a different typeface for your signature line.

Writer's name and job title

Organization's name and contact details

Disclaimer

SIGNING OFF ▶

Signature text saves you the hassle of typing in your personal and business details every time you write an e-mail.

John Doe, Head of Corporate Finance
Largecorp
Tel: +1 212 555 1212
Fax: + 1 212 555 1213
http://www.largecorp.com/
The information in this internet e-mail and any attachments is confidential.
If you are not the intended recipient please notify the sender immediately and do not show this e-mail to anyone else.

USING DIFFERENT E-MAIL ADDRESSES

It is possible to use the same e-mail address for personal and business e-mail, but it is generally easier—and more appropriate— to have separate addresses. Understanding the types of e-mail accounts available will help you to choose a suitable one.

43 Use a web-based provider to create your personal e-mail account.

44 Tell friends to use your personal, not work, account.

▼ **USING PERSONAL E-MAIL WISELY**
A person with a professional attitude does not allow personal e-mail time to eat into official e-mail time.

SEPARATING OFFICIAL AND PERSONAL E-MAIL

Employees should be discouraged from using their work e-mail accounts for personal e-mail. Personal messages can interrupt work flow and create difficulties if an employee is on vacation or leaves the organization. An e-mail with the company's name can also be seen as official communication even if the sender has expressed personal views. Creating a separate personal e-mail account rules out such problems.

UNPROFESSIONAL ATTITUDE | PROFESSIONAL ATTITUDE

Uses work account for personal matters

Sets up personal e-mail account

Mixes work and personal news in same mail

Keeps work and personal accounts separate

Wastes office time checking personal mail

Avoids checking personal account in the office

ORGANIZING MAILBOXES BY JOB ROLE

It often makes sense to provide mailboxes tied to job functions as well as (or instead of) mailboxes for each employee. This is particularly useful when e-mail addresses are published on websites. If your contacts are in the habit of e-mailing sales@yourcompany.com instead of typing in stephen.tan@yourcompany.com, they will not have to change their address books if Mr. Tan is promoted or goes on vacation. If you have more than one role in a company, you can tell from the sender's address and the subject line what the e-mail's content is likely to be. Also, listing multiple addresses by "department" on your website can make your organization seem larger than it is.

THINGS TO DO

1. Use remote access built into your office's e-mail system.
2. Copy in your office account when replying from home.
3. Update office mail against replies sent from home.

45 Redirect a former employee's address to their successor.

▼ MAKING TIME FOR PERSONAL E-MAILS

Sometimes sharing an interesting or amusing e-mail with a colleague can lighten the mood during a stressful day, but only check your personal e-mail account during break periods.

Employee shows his colleague an interesting e-mail, sent to his personal account by a friend

Selecting an E-mail Account

There are three kinds of e-mail services available. **Local server-based e-mail** is provided in medium and large organizations. The servers storing and managing e-mail are within the organization, with "gateways" to the internet. **Standard internet e-mail** ("POP3" or "IMAP") is offered by internet service providers to individuals when they sign up. E-mail is stored on a central server owned by the internet service provider. **Web-based free e-mail** is made available by a third party such as Microsoft's Hotmail or Yahoo Mail. Select different types of e-mail accounts for personal and professional use.

46 Use a web-based e-mail system when office e-mail is not working.

47 Use "POP3" e-mail for easy access if you are using a cellular phone.

Comparing E-Mail Accounts

Types	Advantages	Disadvantages
Local Server-Based E-Mail	● Works quickly and less expensively ● Can handle large amounts of data ● Locally backed up and administered ● More secure ● Easy to monitor e-mail use	● Hard to set up initially ● Requires administration through people and computers within the organization
Standard Internet E-Mail	● Easy to set up ● Easy to use	● Depends on reliability of Internet provider; open to interception ● Requires internet connection to send even internal messages ● Difficult to ensure that business-critical e-mail is backed up
Web-Based Free E-Mail	● Easy to set up ● Free service for low use ● Can be accessed anywhere ● Can be used to divert junk mail ● Easy to use filters ● May prescan for viruses	● Takes longer to get connected ● May appear unprofessional ● Messages cannot be downloaded and then read ● Size of files restricted ● Limited access to technical help

SETTING UP PERSONAL ACCOUNTS

Personal accounts are easy to set up—there are hundreds of free e-mail providers you can access over the internet. You can select any name for your e-mail address, unless it is already taken. You also have the option of setting up two accounts—using one only for your close friends and family. However, when setting up your account you will be asked for certain personal information that may be used by others to send unsolicited mail.

48 Save on phone bills by working off-line whenever possible.

▼ **LENDING CREDIBILITY**
It is useful to own your domain name if you are based at home—this can give your business a more professional image.

POINTS TO REMEMBER

● When working from the office, a direct connection to the company e-mail system should be used.

● Web-based free Internet accounts can be deleted by the provider if they are not used frequently enough.

● Small e-mail providers are less frequently targeted by spammers.

● Multiple e-mail account holders should indicate the purpose of each in the signature line.

OWNING YOUR DOMAIN NAME

Even if you do not have a website, it is still worth owning your organization's own domain name. Without one, your e-mail will have the internet provider's name on it—for instance, yourname@aol.com—instead of your company's name. Not only does this look less professional, but if you change internet providers in the future your e-mail address will also change and you will have to inform all your contacts. If you own a domain name, your e-mail should always come to you, even if you change service providers.

ARCHIVING E-MAIL

There may be times when you delete an e-mail and then find later that you need the information it contained. However, even "deleted" e-mail is not removed permanently from your computer, and there are ways to retrieve it.

49 Find out how long you are required to keep your old e-mail.

RETRIEVING DELETED E-MAILS

In most e-mail systems, when you delete a message, it is moved from the folder it was in to the "trash" or "deleted items" folder. From there, depending on the way your software is set up, it may be removed when you close the program, at the end of a time period, or when the amount of e-mail stored in your account (including "deleted" e-mail) exceeds a certain amount. Check the settings of your e-mail program to make sure that you know how it is set up.

Manager receives complaint from client regarding a delayed order and questions employee about it

Employee searches mailbox for relevant e-mail

Employee has deleted e-mail from mailbox

50 Know your organization's policy on deleting e-mails.

▲ **KEEPING RECORDS**
Archiving e-mail is vital in certain situations. Here, despite being informed by e-mail ahead of time that an order would be delayed, a client sends a complaint to the organization.

MANAGING YOUR ARCHIVES

Some e-mail systems automatically remove old e-mail, but it is better to take control yourself. If you have e-mail you may need in future, create a new folder and store it there. If your office e-mail is held on a central server, you can protect your e-mail from accidental permanent deletion by using the archive function to save that folder to your own hard disk.

Client realizes it was his mistake and withdraws complaint; manager is satisfied with employee

Employee retrieves archived e-mail that proves client had agreed to the delay

E-mail is forwarded to manager and client

Employee is unable to disprove angry client's claim

Manager holds employee responsible for loss of client

AVOIDING E-MAIL BUILDUP

Keeping every e-mail you have sent or received can lead to e-mail mountains. Looking for the deleted message you need amid hundreds of others wastes time. Some e-mail systems store attached files on a central e-mail server—a single attached file can use as much space on a mail server as a hundred simple text messages. Instead, save attached files on your hard disk and delete them from the e-mail system.

51 Request a lost e-mail from the original sender.

PRACTICING SAFE E-MAIL

However careful you are, you will always receive unwanted e-mail. While spam is just annoying, viruses can cause damage. Establish safe working practices and use the correct software to avoid receiving or spreading spam, viruses, and hoaxes.

52 Avoid all business with spammers, however tempting an offer sounds.

53 Never respond to spam—even to ask for it to be deleted.

54 Be careful about giving your e-mail address to forums online.

SHARING YOUR ADDRESS

Many websites will ask for your e-mail address in order to send you a newsletter, or ask you to register before they will show you their material. Somewhere on the form where you fill in your address, you should be asked if you want your e-mail address to be shared with other partner companies. If you leave this box checked, some organizations will feel free to circulate your address widely. If you are not even asked for permission, you risk having your e-mail address shared with anyone for any reason. Such a mistake can often lead to a flood of unsolicited spam.

▼ RECEIVING SPAM
Spammers can take the e-mail address you have registered at websites and then flood you with unwanted mail.

You register your address on an organization's website

Your address is taken from the website by spammers

Spam e-mail starts to come to you from all quarters

Filtering Out Unwanted Mail

Some e-mail software includes built-in filters to automatically remove suspected spam; in others you can produce your own filters. But since spam is always changing, fixed filters are difficult to keep up to date. Add-on software that updates itself automatically and runs either on your own e-mail server, or that provided by your ISP, is also available. It is best to tackle spam as it comes into your organization. In large companies, this is the job of the IT department. However, do check filtered-out e-mail from time to time to ensure that wanted e-mail has not been discarded.

55 Keep up to date with the latest spam techniques.

56 Be cautious about sending commercial e-mail—you may be considered a spammer yourself.

Avoiding Spam

If you put your e-mail addresses on your organization's website, automated searchers may read them and send you unwanted e-mail. Instead, put forms on your web page that forward messages to the right mailbox, or paraphrase your address so that people can interpret it but computers cannot, for instance, by writing (at) instead of @.

Recognizing and Filtering Spam

What to Look For	Significance
Address	The return address is often obviously false, or has a series of numbers instead of a normal e-mail address.
Subject Line	Often in capitals and containing exclamation points. Sometimes contain the text "ADV" (advertisement) and letters or numbers.
Subject	These are "teasers" such as, "Hey, it's me!" or promises of wealth. Words are misspelled to make it hard to delete automatically.
Images	Unlike legitimate messages, spam often has embedded images. Look for "IMG" in the body of the message.
Name	Usually a string of letters or numbers instead of a name and last name in the "From" line.

RECOGNIZING HOAXES AND CHAIN LETTERS

Chain letters and e-mail virus hoax warnings are not dangerous, but they waste office time—particularly when sent to a large number of people. E-mail petitions or invitations to "Send an e-mail and win a prize" are almost always a waste of time. There are websites that keep up to date with the latest versions of these messages. You can search on the internet, either for the text of the e-mail or for "e-mail hoax," to see if the mail you have received is a known hoax. If you are sent a warning about a virus, do not forward it to others unless you are sure it is genuine.

57 Learn to recognize hoaxes quickly to avoid wasting time.

58 Keep antivirus software up to date.

POINTS TO REMEMBER

● If you need to give a website your e-mail address, you can create an alternative address with a web-based e-mail provider.

● To check if your e-mail address has been taken by a company and used unethically, you can "feed" the site with a new e-mail address and monitor the messages there.

● It is important to seek advice about a suspected virus the moment you discover it.

AVOIDING VIRUSES

Computer viruses transmitted through e-mails are becoming more common. Nearly all virus e-mails have attachments, which you are often encouraged to open. Subject lines and the text within tend to be vague and enticing, such as, "Thought you should see this." Do not open any attachment if you are uncertain of its content. The e-mails may seem to come from friends, but the address may be forged. In some cases the senders may not intend to infect you with a virus, and may not realize they have the virus themselves.

59 Remember, a virus may be transmitted unintentionally.

**INFORMING THE ▶
IT DEPARTMENT**
The IT departments of most organizations are equipped to deal with viruses and will get to work as soon as they are informed.

CASE STUDY

Lydia, a small business owner, received an e-mail from a customer with the subject line stating "Virus immunity." The e-mail contained an attached file and instructions to run that file to protect the computer from a dangerous virus. Lydia was suspicious because, to her knowledge, the customer was not an expert in Internet security, and it was highly unlikely that he would send a file of this nature. She went to the website of the provider of her antivirus software, downloaded the latest update available, and scanned the file that had been sent to her. She identified the virus (which had been spread since the last time she updated the software) and removed it before it could infect her computer and cause damage. She then warned the customer that his computer may have also been infected by the virus.

◀ **ELIMINATING A VIRUS YOURSELF**
In this example, a business owner took action on her own when confronted with a virus, and averted a potential crisis.

DEALING WITH A SUSPECTED VIRUS

An e-mail virus can cause immense damage to your and your organization's computer systems. Act immediately if you suspect you have received one and notify the IT department, which runs the organization's computer systems. Dealing with a virus requires specialized knowledge, so do not take any steps to get rid of it yourself—you may simply compound the damage. File the e-mail into a "suspect e-mail" folder. Do not even send it to your IT department, unless they request a copy. Do not restart your computer until you have received instructions from IT support staff or an expert. Do not send a company-wide virus warning—this is the task of your IT department.

60 Be aware that the most popular e-mail packages are more likely to be targeted by virus-writers.

CONTAINING A VIRUS

Receive suspect e-mail

Do not open attachment

Do not forward to others

Notify IT department

Delete from inbox

Delete from system

FOLLOWING NETIQUETTE

There are differences between e-mail and traditional means of communication. Follow these guidelines to compose e-mails that create the right impression, and enhance customer relations.

COMPOSING WITH CARE

The ease with which you can write and send an e-mail encourages informality. This can be beneficial, but can also lead to sloppiness. It is important to take the time to write clearly worded e-mails in order to avoid confusing or offending your recipient.

61 Keep your sentences crisp and differentiate points clearly.

POSITIVE EFFECT   **NEGATIVE EFFECT**

Is baffled by badly composed e-mail

Quickly reads key points

▲ **BEING CONCISE**
Long-winded and convoluted messages are not only irritating, but they also often fail to get your point across effectively.

KEEPING IT SHORT

When writing an e-mail, it is tempting to include everything you know about the subject as it comes to mind. Remember that your e-mail is only one of dozens that each recipient may have to read each day, so it needs to be well-written to catch and retain their attention. Also, if you write a message that takes five minutes to read and you send it to 25 people, it adds up to over two hours of other people's time. Always remember that it is easier to read text on-screen if it is in short paragraphs.

MAKING THE SUBJECT CLEAR

If you want your e-mail to be read, the single most important element is the subject line. Rather than trying to sum up your e-mail at the start, write the body of your e-mail first, then read through it and try to sum it up. Do not write very long subject lines—keep in mind that a subject line that is too long may not be displayed fully in many people's e-mail inboxes.

62 Avoid using more than 50 characters in the subject line.

▼ **WRITING SUCCINCTLY**
Learn to write e-mails that are easy to read, get your message across clearly, and do not take up people's time unnecessarily.

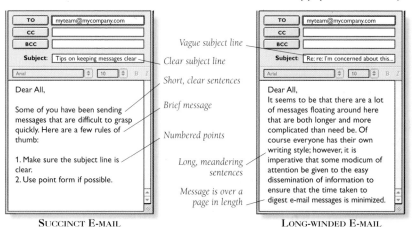

Vague subject line
Clear subject line
Short, clear sentences
Brief message
Numbered points
Long, meandering sentences
Message is over a page in length

SUCCINCT E-MAIL

LONG-WINDED E-MAIL

Succinct e-mail body:

Dear All,

Some of you have been sending messages that are difficult to grasp quickly. Here are a few rules of thumb:

1. Make sure the subject line is clear.
2. Use point form if possible.

Long-winded e-mail body:

Dear All,
It seems to be that there are a lot of messages floating around here that are both longer and more complicated than need be. Of course everyone has their own writing style; however, it is imperative that some modicum of attention be given to the easy dissemination of information to ensure that the time taken to digest e-mail messages is minimized.

HANDLING REPLIES

Keep the subject line (normally starting with "Re:") the same when replying to someone else's message. This helps when you file the e-mail sequence later. Shorten or delete a chain of "Re: Re:" text before any e-mail. When replying, put general comments at the top, comment on specific issues alongside the relevant text, and delete any nonessential information. Avoid just adding your comments at the top. If this happens repeatedly, the e-mail can grow to unreadable lengths.

THINGS TO DO

1. To avoid courtesy replies, use NRN (no reply neccessary).

2. If all you have to say can be contained in the subject line, use EOM (end of message) to indicate that the e-mail need not be opened.

COMMUNICATING CLEARLY

Unlike letters, e-mails are usually informal, and often chatty in tone. However, some recipients may misread or misinterpret your message. Keep your recipients in mind when writing, and maintain some formality until you know them well.

63 Write simply— not all recipients will share your mother tongue.

64 Use abbreviations only if you are sure the recipient can understand them.

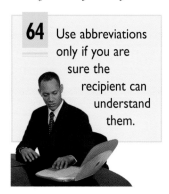

ABBREVIATING WORDS

E-mail is increasingly composed on the move, sometimes using telephone number pads instead of normal keyboards. To avoid having to type long words, phone users have constructed a language of occasionally cryptic abbreviations. Some Internet users also resort to similar abbreviations—for example, typing "AFAIK" instead of "as far as I know." Use this language only if you are comfortable with it. Avoid using such "coded" language on strangers unless you know the recipient is familiar with it.

KNOWING WHEN TO ADD SMILEYS

In the early days of e-mail, a form of shorthand was developed that aimed to add interest and humor to messages. Smileys are faces made of punctuation marks and can be used to indicate the tone of the preceding text. There are many variations, but the most basic ones are explained here. However, these symbols are not universally understood, and many people find them childish. Avoid using smileys in business communication, unless the person you are communicating with uses them first.

UNDERSTANDING SMILEYS

SMILEY	MEANING
:-)	The basic smiley—usually indicates happiness.
;-)	Winking—usually indicates a joke or (sometimes) flirtatiousness.
:-(	Frowning—usually indicates sadness or disagreement.
:-I	Indifferent—usually indicates apathy or disinterest.
:->	Sarcastic—usually indicates insincerity or cynicism.

ADDRESSING RECIPIENTS

When writing an e-mail to someone for the first time, it is difficult to know how to address them and how to sign off. Until you have communicated several times, it is best to retain a formal tone by addressing people as "Dear (name)" and sign off "Sincerely." Signing off with "Regards" is usually considered more informal—only use it if you are friendly with the recipient.

65 Resolve emotional disagreements face to face or by phone if possible.

66 Avoid sarcasm or irony in all business e-mails.

▼ **SEEKING ADVICE**
When you are under stress, it is a good idea to get another opinion on the e-mail you have written. Show it to someone who is not involved in the dispute before making up your mind about sending it.

CURBING EMOTIONS

Think carefully before sending messages when you are angry or upset. You may think your message is calm and reasonable but your emotion may reveal itself inappropriately. It is often difficult to write in a measured fashion when you are feeling agitated for any reason. What you think is a strongly worded complaint may be read as a furious rant by the recipient. If in any doubt, leave your message unsent for a while, return to it later, and re-read it in a calmer frame of mind.

Sender asks for a second opinion

Neutral person suggests a few changes

MAKING FILES READABLE

You can send many different types of files as attachments to e-mail. However, as there are many variations in the type of software available, it is important to send files in the smallest form possible, and check that your recipient will be able to open them.

67 Use plain text instead of attaching files wherever possible.

68 Find out which programs are used by those you e-mail regularly.

69 Use the JPEG format to send an image file.

FORMATTING E-MAILS

Many e-mail programs allow you to format your messages by changing the font, style, size, or color of text, or by inserting bullet points and tables, and so on. These features are often useful inside office environments where everyone has the same e-mail program. However, not all programs have this capability, and those that do are sometimes not compatible with each other. Unless you know your recipient is using the same e-mail package as you are, it is best to send your message as "plain text." Keep in mind, however, that this may require you to edit your software's settings.

KEEPING IT SMALL

Most files can be e-mailed on an inter-office network. However, when you send a file out of the office, make sure it is not too large for the recipient's computer to cope with. The recipient's e-mail connection may be through a modem, in which case a file of, say, one megabyte, which took you just a few seconds to send, could take the recipient over 15 minutes to pick up. Some office networks limit the size of attached files they will accept, and some recipients may pick up their messages on a mobile phone, which can be many times slower than a desktop computer. Always use a compression program on larger files before sending them. If necessary, tell the recipient how to uncompress the file.

◄ MODEMS VARY
Older modems can take up to two minutes to download a file of just 100Kb.

SENDING ATTACHMENTS

In addition to a simple e-mail message, you may want to send an image or document as a file attachment. Before you do this, ensure that your recipient's software is capable of opening the file. You may assume that they have some form of Microsoft Office, or Office-compatible software, for example. However, they may not be able to read your document if you have the latest version while theirs is several years old. If in doubt, open the document, then save it again using "save as" instead of "save," and choose an earlier version of your software. It is unlikely you will lose any important formatting—you should be warned if formatting is affected in any way.

70 Ensure compatibility with others by using the most popular software to create attachments.

DOS AND DON'TS

✔ Do use a compression program such as Win-Zip when attaching a large document.

✔ Do use Adobe's Acrobat program to create files that most software can read.

✔ Do make sure that the files you send end in an appropriate code, such as ".doc."

✔ Do be aware of the size of the attachment you are sending.

✘ Don't send attachments over 1Mb in size without warning the recipient.

✘ Don't give generic names to attachments, since this makes them harder to file.

✘ Don't forward attachments if you only need to comment on an e-mail's text.

✘ Don't use a colored background or text— it can be hard to read.

Wastes time waiting for an uncompressed file to download

◄ COMPRESSING FILES

When sending file attachments, make sure that you compress them. Large, uncompressed files take time to download, hold up work, and cause irritation to the recipient.

ADDRESSING THE WORLD

When sending an e-mail to someone abroad, it is easy to assume they are just like you. Bear in mind that they may not read your language well, may not have the same level of internet access, or may have a different attitude toward the medium.

> **71** Avoid complex sentences and jargon when composing e-mail.

CULTURAL DIFFERENCES

In Asian countries, recipients may expect a formally composed message—first names are not always used, unless the sender is quite familiar with the recipient. This may seem overly reserved to people in North America or the UK, where a more informal approach is usually acceptable.

TRANSLATING E-MAILS

The Internet has ceased to be an English-only medium—nearly two-thirds of Internet users do not speak English as their first language, and that proportion is growing. Web-based translation tools and downloadable software are available to translate between languages word by word. This can be useful to get a general idea of what the message says when an e-mail arrives in a different language, but cannot be relied on for long messages as the results are likely to be garbled. It is much better to get someone who speaks the language to translate for you.

◀ **E-MAILING GLOBALLY**
In today's global market, language is no longer considered to be a barrier. There are easy electronic facilities available for quick, basic translation.

> **72** If you receive e-mail in an unfamiliar language, alert the sender.

KEEPING INTERNET RATES IN MIND

If you are sending e-mail to developing countries, remember that internet access may be very costly—in countries such as Bangladesh, monthly internet charges can be higher than the average monthly income, while in the US they are as little as one percent. In many countries, internet access is charged by the minute and the speed of a connection may be very slow. As a result, e-mail accounts may not be checked often, and large files may cause a bottleneck.

73 Use the recipient's title, such as Dr., in your message.

74 Write formally to an overseas client for the first time.

75 Bear in mind any time difference with the recipient's country or city.

Knows the accepted
e-mailing conventions of
different countries

Finds out
the best
time to send
an e-mail

Checks
if recipient
understands
message

Has a
global outlook

Writes
clear, concise
e-mails

BEING AWARE ▶
*To be effective when communicating
overseas by e-mail, you need to find
out the e-mail culture of the
countries to which you send
messages regularly.*

QUESTIONS TO ASK YOURSELF

Q Do I know the correct way to address everyone I send e-mail to all over the world?

Q Do I take into account other people's e-mailing habits when corresponding with them?

Q Am I aware of the level of internet access in my recipient's country?

KNOWING THE TIME ZONES

E-mail may travel the globe almost instantly, but the world is at work in different time zones. If you send an e-mail from New York to London in the afternoon, do not expect an answer that day—the recipients may have already left the office. Time zones can also work to your advantage. If you send an urgent message from New York to London at the end of your day, the recipients can work on the problem for five hours while you sleep.

MEETING CUSTOMERS' NEEDS

Using e-mail has made communication with customers easier, but if badly implemented, it can be a source of frustration for them. Ensure that your organization is responsive to customer e-mail, and keep e-mail marketing sensitive to customer needs.

76 Remember that customers usually expect a reply to e-mail within a day.

77 Provide e-mail addresses on all promotional literature.

PROVIDING YOUR E-MAIL ADDRESS

Put e-mail addresses on business cards, your company stationery, and all promotional literature. Also make sure relevant e-mail addresses are available from your company's website. Allocate appropriate e-mail addresses to your employees— for instance, an invoice should have the address of the accounts department, a sales brochure should have the sales address, and so on—this saves you having to forward e-mails internally.

▼ MANAGING EXPECTATIONS
Monitor staff and colleagues to ensure timely responses to e-mails. Remember, urgent work needs an urgent response. In this example, the customer's opinion of the organization depends on the manager's response to his e-mail.

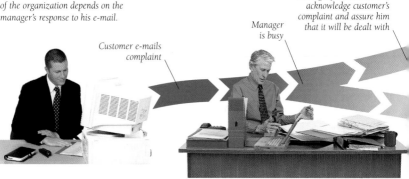

Customer e-mails complaint

Manager is busy

Manager finds the time to acknowledge customer's complaint and assure him that it will be dealt with

78 Add details about how to unsubscribe in any newsletter.

CIRCULATING E-MAIL NEWSLETTERS

E-mail newsletters can be an invaluable way of marketing your organization to customers who have asked to stay in touch. Not only do these cost little to send, they can be passed on for easy word-of-mouth referrals. While customers may forget to return to your website, an e-mail arriving in their mailbox regularly is an easy way to remind them of new products and services. It is a good way to obtain feedback, since customers can reply instantly. However, always ask before adding anyone to your newsletter mailing list.

Customer appreciates the quick response and his relationship with the organization is strengthened

79 Acknowledge a customer e-mail, even if you cannot reply in full immediately.

Responsiblity is delegated to junior

Customer feels angry at being ignored and takes his business away

Customer's complaint lies unanswered

MANAGING MAILING LISTS

If you regularly contact many people with the same e-mail, consider using mailing list software instead of a regular e-mail package. This will allow recipients to sign up or remove themselves from the list automatically. You can also reach a larger number of people on a single list. There are several web-based mailing list options including yahoogroups.com (free, if you allow them to add advertising), or you can buy the software and install and use it yourself if your company is always connected to the Internet.

80 Avoid sending newsletters more than once a week.

81 Address recipients of your marketing e-mail by name.

CUSTOMIZING YOUR E-MAIL

When you send marketing e-mail, it is well worth making the effort to customize your message. You can maintain a few standard e-mail newsletters with different offers aimed at different customers. However, with the right mailing list software, you can be more selective, automatically sending different offers to different recipients based on their ZIP code, age, gender, or other criteria. However, to make this work, you must gather this information by asking those who want to sign up to provide some basic details about themselves.

▼ **SENDING E-MAIL TO THE RIGHT PEOPLE**
Few people today will bother to wade through piles of promotional material. Direct your e-mail marketing to catch each customer's attention.

Customized newsletter is printed out and read with interest

Recipient deletes noncustomized newsletter unread

POSITIVE OUTCOME NEGATIVE OUTCOME

INTRODUCING CUSTOMERS TO EACH OTHER

Normally corporate newsletters only allow customers to send a response to the company sending them out. However, with careful handling, "open" mailing lists—where customers can contact all other recipients by replying—can also be useful. In this way customers can help each other use your product. If they can answer each others' questions, it helps your support team. You also gain insights into the improvements that customers would like to see.

82 Gather information from other organizations' messageboards.

▼ NETWORKING EASILY
E-mail newsletters and messageboards are crucial aids for keeping you and your clients informed and in touch with each other.

Alerts customers to special promotions

Gives you information about customer needs and problems

Warns customers about product changes

Helps you target specific customer interests

Informs customers about upcoming offers

Allows customer interaction

QUESTIONS TO ASK YOURSELF

Q Will my customers be willing to help each other?

Q How would my organization handle criticism voiced publicly through our mailing lists?

Q Is someone available in my company to participate sensitively in online discussion?

Q Can the company effectively use the information it gathers?

USING MESSAGEBOARDS

Free or inexpensive software is also available to add messageboard facilities to your website. If your open mailing list is becoming too busy for customers to follow, a messageboard may be simpler to manage. It is easier to scan through 100 messages in one place than to open and read 100 e-mails in your inbox. Messages posted to the messageboard are visible indefinitely (until removed), so customers who want an answer to a question can find it there instead of having to e-mail you directly.

MAINTAINING E-MAIL POLICY

Organizations need clear policies about e-mail security and abuse. Follow these policies, and make sure employees are aware of them, to protect your organization from legal threats.

KEEPING TRACK OF YOUR E-MAIL RECIPIENTS

Normally, of course, the only people who will read a message you send are yourself and the recipients. However, other people can get hold of those messages. You should be aware of the ways in which they can do this, and how to guard against it.

82 Check that all names are correct if you are e-mailing several people.

83 Never send an e-mail you would not want to see in the news next day.

GUARDING YOUR PRIVACY

Messages sent inside your organization are fairly safe from interception from outside the office, but when a message enters the Internet, your privacy cannot always be guaranteed. Your own Internet provider, the recipients' Internet providers, and determined hackers may be able to read e-mails you send that have not been encrypted (scrambled) in some way. In practice, this rarely occurs, but you should be aware of the risk.

UNDERSTANDING THE DANGERS

Sometimes an e-mail can end up being read by someone for whom it was not intended. The person you send an e-mail to may be away, leaving someone else to handle their e-mail, or you may accidentally send an e-mail to the wrong person. Most dangerously, the message you sent can be forwarded by the recipient to anyone they like. Worse still, they can edit the e-mail before sending, so that the sense or content of your message is completely changed.

▲ DELETING E-MAIL

An e-mail, once sent, is difficult to delete. Even if you remove it from your computer, it may have been archived from the central server. Usually there is no way of removing it from the recipient's inbox short of asking the recipient to do so.

CASE STUDY

A manager in a software company received a puzzled e-mail from a customer who had begun to receive internal memos of the organization. He investigated the matter and discovered how this had happened—the customer's name was similar to the name of one of the sales staff and had been added to an internal e-mail list in error. The manager checked the internal mail that had been sent to the customer and determined that no critical information had escaped. He made sure that the customer's name was deleted from the internal e-mail list. The manager then circulated an e-mail to the rest of the staff, drawing their attention to the incident. In it, he stressed the importance of employees cross-checking the recipients' names and addresses before sending mails.

◀ BEING CAREFUL

In this example, potential problems arising out of the sales department's carelessness in sending internal e-mail were averted only because the accidental recipient was honest.

MONITORING E-MAIL

Governments have been increasingly monitoring e-mails in the interests of prevention of terrorism and other crime. It is unlikely that they are reading your e-mail unless you are in a sensitive industry, but spy agencies may keep an eye on the overall flow of traffic between organizations in which they are interested. So, if you exchange e-mail with a company that in turn exchanges messages with an organization under suspicion, your own e-mail could come under scrutiny.

SECURING E-MAIL

Given the risks of interception or misdirection of e-mail, some confidential documents will need additional protection. Use effective passwords and software to ensure that sensitive e-mails are seen by only the intended recipients.

84 Use internal networks for best security in e-mail between offices.

85 Attach password-protected files instead of sending text e-mails.

▼ **DISCLOSING PASSWORDS**
Many employers insist that at least one key person knows all the passwords. If you have to divulge your password to someone, do so in person.

USING PASSWORDS

The simplest way to protect a file is to attach a password to it. However, passwords need to be chosen and used carefully to prevent them from being guessed by others. For example, instead of using words, you may find it useful to use the initial letters of a phrase. Passwords should never be written down, and should be changed at regular intervals. Find out your organization's policy on sharing passwords, and ensure that you reveal your passwords only to authorized IT personnel.

ENFORCING SECURITY

Most security breaches do not occur because hackers use powerful computers to break into computer systems. Leaks often come from inside an organization, perpetrated by people using passwords they are authorized to have or that they are able to work out or acquire. Competitors can contact your staff and impersonate a member of the IT department to obtain passwords. The most sophisticated security software will not protect your data if the security discipline is lax.

86 Take the passwords for secured files from employees who leave.

▼ **DEVISING PASSWORDS**
Choose passwords that cannot be easily worked out by others. There are various ways you can do this.

Substitute letters for words	Use deliberate misspellings	Use a language your co-workers do not speak

DOS AND DON'TS

✔ Do change passwords frequently.

✔ Do choose unusual passwords that cannot be easily guessed.

✔ Do make sure that security software is kept up to date.

✘ Don't discard surplus computers without removing all data.

✘ Don't use the same password many times.

✘ Don't pick passwords based on personal facts that others can guess.

ENCRYPTING E-MAIL

The most sophisticated way to securely send files across the Internet is to use encryption, the most popular form being "public key" encryption. Add-on software for this facility is available for most personal computer e-mail software, but while it is powerful, it tends to be complicated to install and use. The recipient has to use the same kind of software, and for them to read your e-mail they need two "keys" (or passwords)—one public (hence "public key" encryption) and one private. This can make it too cumbersome for routine use.

GUARDING AGAINST HACKERS

Even encrypted files are not 100 percent safe. If your organization does not always use encryption, then the very fact that a file is encrypted will draw attention to it. Determined hackers can probably get through most security measures. You can only hope to make their job more difficult.

87 Test internal security practices regularly and without warning.

Avoiding Legal Pitfalls

From a legal perspective, e-mail turns everyone in your company into a publisher. The fact that all e-mail is recorded and can be produced in court raises the specter of legal threats. Reduce this danger by practicing safe e-mailing techniques.

88 Remember that an employer can be prosecuted for an employee's error.

89 Warn recipients if an e-mail is confidential.

90 Consult a lawyer if you fear you may face legal action.

STAYING ON THE RIGHT SIDE OF THE LAW

Be careful about making critical comments about other companies by e-mail. Factual statements, such as "our products are less expensive" are acceptable, if true. However, if you cast doubts on an organizations integrity or financial stability, you could be subject to legal action, and the injured party need not prove the statements are false to win the case—you would have to prove your statements are true. Even messages sent only inside your organization are potentially libelous.

CASE STUDY

An employee working in a multinational organization heard a rumor that the company's rival was in serious financial trouble. He forwarded an e-mail containing this information to some of his colleagues, who in turn forwarded it to others in the company.

As the information began to circulate internally by e-mail, it came to the notice of a senior-level manager who alerted the legal department. The department was concerned the rival could hear about the e-mail. If that occurred, the company could be sued for defamation. They circulated an e-mail to everyone in the office warning against forwarding the rumor, either internally or outside the organization. The IT department was asked to delete all of the e-mails on the subject from the company servers, an order that was promptly carried out.

◀ **PROTECTING THE ORGANIZATION**
In this example, timely intervention from the legal department averted a potential lawsuit for defamation that might have cost the company heavy damages.

CARELESS CONDUCT | CAREFUL CONDUCT

Is unaware of legal aspects of e-mail

Keeps up with laws relating to e-mail

Is casual in writing e-mails

Carefully words even internal e-mail

Indiscriminately forwards sensitive e-mail

Takes care to delete inappropriate e-mail

GUARDING AGAINST LIABILITY

Contracts are formed not only on paper—if you agree to something by e-mail, it may constitute a legally binding contract, even if you are not actually the person in your company authorized to make such a decision. What matters is that the recipient could reasonably believe that you had the authority to make the decision. Avoid making promises or agreements via e-mail, unless you are certain that it is safe to do so.

▲ BEING AWARE
One e-mail from a careless employee can cause huge damage to a company. All employees need to be aware of the legal ramifications of e-mail.

91 Ask permission before forwarding sensitive e-mail.

QUESTIONS TO ASK YOURSELF

Q Do I have access to legal advice if needed?

Q Does my team understand the legal risks and responsibilities of e-mail?

Q Do I adequately monitor employee e-mail to prevent illegal actions?

Q Am I adequately insured against lawsuits?

BREACHING CONFIDENCE

If someone sends confidential business information to your company by e-mail, and your employees forward it on to another, unauthorized source, your company can be held responsible for the resulting breach of confidence, even if it was unintentional. To prevent your own confidential material from being passed on inadvertently, ensure sensitive documents are properly labeled as such. If you want to provide extra protection, you can ask recipients to agree to a nondisclosure agreement before you release confidential information.

93 Monitoring e-mail seeking image files can prevent misuse.

94 Remember that what seems funny to some may offend others.

POINTS TO REMEMBER

● Staff must be aware that e-mails can be used as evidence in court.

● A sexual harassment charge can cost an organization in both legal settlements and damage to its reputation.

● Find out about marketing and advertising laws of other countries before sending e-mails.

AVOIDING SEXUAL HARASSMENT CLAIMS

Any e-mail containing pornographic images or racy humor can be considered sexual harassment, even when the person who takes the case to court is only one of several people to receive the e-mail. If such e-mail is in general circulation, it can be construed as creating a hostile environment, and even those who do not receive the e-mail can take out a lawsuit against the company for allowing such traffic to occur. Never send jokes or other personal, potentially legally threatening material on company e-mail servers.

▼ **BANNING INDECENT E-MAIL**
Those who send e-mail with inappropriate content are deemed publishers of the material, even if they did not create it themselves. An organization should have a strict policy against staff who use company resources for such e-mails.

Manager warns colleagues that such e-mails are unacceptable

Receives sexist joke via e-mail and shows it to colleague

CULTURAL DIFFERENCES

Laws differ in every country. Even if you are safely within your own laws, you could be held to have broken the laws of the country of the recipient. For example, it is against the law in Germany to offer consumers two items for the price of one, and in Sweden it is illegal to advertise toys to children.

▲ **SEEKING PERMISSION**
Before copying and forwarding research or any other material written by someone else, check that the author is happy for you to do so.

95 Indicate an e-mail's sensitivity at the top of the message.

96 Treat all rule violations as a serious offense.

VIOLATING COPYRIGHT

It is easy to forward the text of research reports and other copyrighted information by e-mail, and those who do so often believe this is permissible. But ownership of a file or document by one person in the company may not give the owner the right to share it freely. There are rights to "fair use" of copyright material for research, but this is often restricted to academic, rather than commercial research. Even when permitted, it normally only allows for the publication of excerpts of the text, not the entire article.

USING E-MAIL DISCLAIMERS

Many people seem to consider that a lengthy disclaimer added automatically to the end of all outgoing e-mail protects them against most legal risks. Such disclaimers can be useful, but they need to be tailored to your company's needs and the sensitivity of each e-mail. If untrue statements are made, disclaimers will not protect you. Phrases such as "this e-mail contains confidential information—if you have received it in error, please inform the sender and delete it" can be useful, but remember that a disclaimer automatically attaches to every e-mail and may lose its impact.

COMMUNICATING E-MAIL POLICIES

It is all too easy for an organization to be sued on the basis of an e-mail that the sender wrote without realizing the wider implications. Make sure everyone you work with knows your organization's policies about e-mail use and misuse.

97 Lobby for an e-mail policy if your organization does not have one.

98 Be aware of e-mail monitoring policies in your workplace.

99 Monitor e-mail to the minimum extent needed.

RESPECTING THE LAW

The law around the world treats e-mail very seriously, and legal battles are proliferating on numerous issues, from libel to "accidental" contracts and sexual harassment. Some organizations scan their employees' e-mails to ensure that the law is not being broken, but in doing so they run the risk of alienating their workers (when they are aware of such monitoring). Inappropriate monitoring can even result in organizations being prosecuted for violating the human rights of their staff.

THINGS TO DO

1. Include efficiency guidelines alongside legal issues.
2. Provide a policy reference guide tailored to your organization's needs.
3. Draw up clear and fair penalties for policy breaches by staff.

Colleague notes down particular points of relevance

Legal advisor called in for her opinion

CREATING RULES

Research the e-mail policy of other organizations

Draw up a staff e-mail policy

Communicate the new policy to staff

KNOWING THE POLICY

Your company may already have e-mail policies in place. If you were not aware of one but you subsequently discover it, you should urge the organization to make it more widely known—if it is not known among all the employees, it cannot be effective in changing their behavior, and if it involves e-mail monitoring but is not public, it may be illegal. Whether or not this policy is applied across the organization, ask if you can devise a specific e-mail policy to suit the requirements of your team.

100 Make policy briefing part of new staff training.

101 Ensure that staff understand why the policy is in place.

▼ **MAKING THE POLICY CLEAR**
An e-mail policy will not be effective unless it is explained clearly. It is worth organizing workshops to make employees aware of the legal risks involved in e-mail.

Manager uses hypothetical examples drawn from his own field to illustrate the legal aspects of e-mail

Colleague appreciates the responsibility involved in writing an e-mail

Assessing Your E-mailing Skills

Effective use of e-mail is not something you can learn in a day. Evaluate your performance by responding to the following statements, marking the option closest to your experience. Be as honest as you can. If your answer is "never," mark Option 1; if it is "always," mark Option 4, and so on. Add your scores together, and refer to the analysis to see how you scored and to identify areas that need improvement.

Options	
1 Never	
2 Occasionally	
3 Frequently	
4 Always	

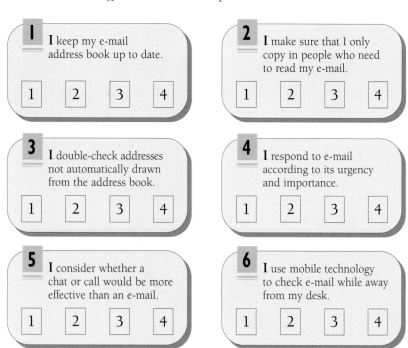

1 I keep my e-mail address book up to date.

1 | 2 | 3 | 4

2 I make sure that I only copy in people who need to read my e-mail.

1 | 2 | 3 | 4

3 I double-check addresses not automatically drawn from the address book.

1 | 2 | 3 | 4

4 I respond to e-mail according to its urgency and importance.

1 | 2 | 3 | 4

5 I consider whether a chat or call would be more effective than an e-mail.

1 | 2 | 3 | 4

6 I use mobile technology to check e-mail while away from my desk.

1 | 2 | 3 | 4

7 I arrange work practices to allow out-of-office working where applicable.

1 2 3 4

8 I sort my incoming and sent e-mail into folders.

1 2 3 4

9 I check my folders to make sure messages have not been misfiled or forgotten.

1 2 3 4

10 I use filters to handle my incoming e-mail.

1 2 3 4

11 I use labels to indicate messages I may need to refer to later.

1 2 3 4

12 I ensure key contacts know when I will be unable to read my e-mail.

1 2 3 4

13 I put contacts that could be useful to others into a shared address book.

1 2 3 4

14 I double-check that an e-mail based on a template is appropriate to the recipient.

1 2 3 4

15 I ensure that the e-mail addresses of new employees are circulated.

1 2 3 4

16 I use a separate account for my personal e-mail.

1 2 3 4

17 I find out the privacy policy of a website before giving it my e-mail address.

1 2 3 4

18 I check junk e-mail filters to ensure that no wanted e-mail has been deleted.

1 2 3 4

19 I avoid forwarding chain letters and virus warnings.

1 2 3 4

20 I ensure that the antivirus software on my computer is up to date.

1 2 3 4

21 I can recognize e-mail that is likely to contain a virus.

1 2 3 4

22 I edit my e-mails to make sure that they are clear and succinct.

1 2 3 4

23 I remove unnecessary text from the original e-mail when I reply to it.

1 2 3 4

24 I make my subject lines concise and clear.

1 2 3 4

25 I avoid jargon—whether related to technology or e-mail.

1 2 3 4

26 I avoid sending e-mail when I am upset or angry.

1 2 3 4

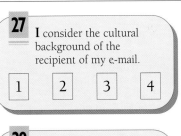

27 I consider the cultural background of the recipient of my e-mail.

| 1 | 2 | 3 | 4 |

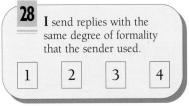

28 I send replies with the same degree of formality that the sender used.

| 1 | 2 | 3 | 4 |

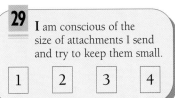

29 I am conscious of the size of attachments I send and try to keep them small.

| 1 | 2 | 3 | 4 |

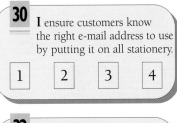

30 I ensure customers know the right e-mail address to use by putting it on all stationery.

| 1 | 2 | 3 | 4 |

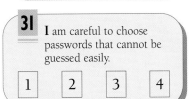

31 I am careful to choose passwords that cannot be guessed easily.

| 1 | 2 | 3 | 4 |

32 I am confident that my co-workers are aware of e-mail use policies.

| 1 | 2 | 3 | 4 |

ANALYSIS

Now that you have completed the self-assessment, add up the total score and check your performance by referring to the corresponding evaluation below. Whatever level of success you have achieved, there is always room for improvement. Focus on any areas of weakness and refer to the sections in this book for guidance.

32–64: You need to work on developing your skills if you are to use e-mail effectively.

65–95: You have sound knowledge of many aspects of e-mail use, whether personal or within your organization. Review remaining areas of weakness to build on your expertise.

96–128: Your grasp of e-mail and its use is good. Share your knowledge with others in your team and focus on refining your skills.

INDEX

ACKNOWLEDGMENTS

AUTHOR'S ACKNOWLEDGMENTS

This book would not have been possible without the hard work of a talented team of professionals. In particular I would like to thank Nicky Munro, Adèle Hayward, and Jude Garlick at DK in London for helping me to organize and present the material effectively and the team in New Delhi for their sterling work in designing and editing the book remotely—a testament to the power of e-mail! Thanks, too, to the people, who introduced me to e-mail—you know who you are—and to my wife, Delphine, whose love and support are, as ever, indispensable.

PUBLISHER'S ACKNOWLEDGMENTS

Dorling Kindersley would like to thank the following for their help and participation in producing this book:

Picture research Kavita Dutta
Picture librarian Richard Dabb
Editorial help Sheema Mookherjee
Indexer Margaret McCormack
Photography Gary Ombler, Steve Gorton, Mathew Ward, Andy Crawford, Tim Ridley

PICTURE CREDITS

Key: *a* above, *b* bottom, *c* center, *l* left, *r* right, *t* top
Corbis: David Katzenstein 4c; Charles Gupton 6; D. Boone 7t; Peter Turnley 14; Dann Tardif 37c; Jose Luis Pelaez, Inc. 50; Bill Varie 58

All other images © Dorling Kindersley.

For further information see: www.dkimages.com

AUTHOR'S BIOGRAPHY

David Brake is a journalist and internet consultant with more than 15 years' experience of e-mail and the internet. He has written for a wide range of print and electronic publications, including the *Daily Telegraph*, BBC News Online, *Personal Computer World*, and *New Scientist*. He has also lectured for the Open University. David's website at www.DavidBrake.org contains further information about e-mail use in organizations.